PROHIBITION COCKTAILS

21 Secrets & Recipes

DENITTA WARD

COPYRIGHT

PRINTED IN THE UNITED STATES OF AMERICA

Welbourne Press
www.welbournepress.com

1st Edition
ISBN-13: 978-0-9993018-2-1

LIBRARY OF CONGRESS CONTROL NO. 2018901040

Copyright ©2018 by Denitta Ward
All rights reserved.

www.denitta.com

Cover Design by FantasyArt
Author Photo by Nicole Jenkins

10 9 8 7 6 5 4 3 2 1

PROHIBITION COCKTAILS

TABLE OF CONTENTS

A BRIEF HISTORY OF PROHIBITION	1
BEE'S KNEES	13
CLOVER CLUB	17
CORPSE REVIVER - ORIGINAL & No. 2	21
DAIQUIRIS: CLASSIC & FRUITY	25
DUBONNET COCKTAIL	29
FRENCH 75	31
GIMLET	35
GIN RICKEY	39
HANKY-PANKY	43
HIGHBALL	47
MARY PICKFORD	49
MINT JULEP	53
MONKEY GLAND	57
PLANTER'S PUNCH	61
SCOFFLAW	65
SIDECAR	69
SOUTH SIDE	73
THE LAST WORD	77
TUXEDO NO. 2	81
TWELVE-MILE LIMIT	85
WARD 8	89
1920s COCKTAIL PARTY PLANNER	93
Also by Denitta Ward	99
About the Author	101
Photo Credits	103

A BRIEF HISTORY OF PROHIBITION

America's "Noble Experiment" from 1920 to 1933

*I*n honor of the 21st Amendment, which ended the United States' ban on the production and sale of liquor, presented here are 21 secrets and recipes of the Prohibition cocktails that have withstood the test of time.

But first, some history.

With Prohibition reigning from 1920 to 1933, liquor was illegal but somehow that did not stop it from being produced and consumed in the United States.

Instead, secret speakeasy bars sprang up across the country, people made their own beer and liquors at home, interstate smuggling of liquor grew, crime syndicates developed, and demand for drink continued. But, good came from the failed experiment.

Creative cocktails were designed or, in some cases, rediscovered during the Prohibition years. The twenty-one best are included here.

WHAT WAS PROHIBITION?

On January 17, 1920, a few simple words added to the Constitution of the United States swept change across the States and throughout communities nationwide. Liquor could not be made or sold.

The 18th Amendment provided:

After one year from the ratification of this article the manufacture, sale, or transportation of intoxicating liquors within, the importation thereof into, or the exportation thereof from the United States and all the territory subject to the jurisdiction thereof for beverage purposes is hereby prohibited.

The 18th Amendment, once passed by Congress, would subsequently be ratified by a majority of states in 1919, with Nebraska voters casting the final ratification vote needed. Prohibition thereby became the law of the land, and drove liquor sales far underground, sometimes quite literally.

Though ratified in 1919, the Prohibition Amendment's actual effective date was not until 1920, which provided a one year period for citizens to build up a stock of alcohol.

Otherwise law-abiding citizens were faced with ethical and moral dilemmas - to adhere to the law and live without alcohol, or to disregard it at their own peril.

The Amendment's language was clear; there was only one problem. Nowhere did the 18th Amendment define exactly what was an "intoxicating liquor."

Without a legal definition, the ban could scarcely be enforced.

Congress needed to then enact legislation defining what beverages would be prohibited. Accompanying the 18th Amendment was the **National Prohibition Act**, commonly known as the **Volstead Act**.

Congress passed the Volstead Act and President Woodrow Wilson vetoed it. Then, a re-vote was taken and on October 28, 1919, the Volstead Act became law after an override of President Wilson's veto.

Mr. Wayne Wheeler of the Anti-Saloon League drafted the National Prohibition Act, and named it for the

Chairman of the House Judiciary Committee, Andrew Volstead.

Volstead himself lost his House seat in 1922 and throughout his life declined, on ethical grounds, opportunities to publicly speak about Prohibition.

Likely aware that the strict and absolute prohibition of liquor would be met with wily and creative ways to circumvent the law, the Volstead Act carved out exceptions to the prohibition on the manufacture, sale and transport of liquors.

One of the biggest loopholes in the Volstead Act was the authorization of prescription liquor.

LIQUOR BY PRESCRIPTION

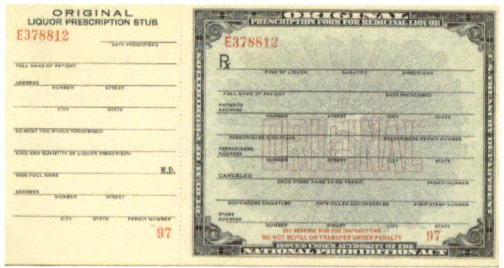

Prescription form for medicinal liquor

Family physicians were allowed to prescribe whiskey and other liquor for patients, to provide a medicinal remedy for their ills, and pharmacies were allowed to fill those prescriptions. Almost overnight, family doctors and local pharmacists (commonly called "druggists" then) became quite popular community citizens. Physicians had full discretion to prescribe, or not prescribe liquor, and druggist could chose whether or not to fill the prescriptions of patent medicine.

HOME CONSUMPTION AND HOME-BREWS

The Volstead Act allowed consumption of alcohol in private residences if the liquor had been acquired prior to Prohibition's effective date. With a year wait until Prohibition's actual effective date, citizens had months to fill their cellars and storehouses.

The law also allowed people to make up to 200 gallons of "non-intoxicating cider and fruit juice" within the privacy of their own home for home consumption.

This exception allowed home-brews, generally ciders or wine, to be made if they were under 0.5% alcohol by volume. It was not uncommon for home-brews to be made even in the best of kitchens across America.

Pabst and Anheuser-Busch ran a brisk business selling malt extract and supplies needed for home-brewing, thus mitigating some of the loss of other income streams.

The wine industry saw a boom. Grape growers saw prices of wine grapes increase from $30/ton to $375/ton. Vineyards sold wine "bricks" of dried grape juice concentrate that could be reconstituted. The bricks included a clear warning that diluting the brick with water and letting it sit in a cupboard for 21 days would turn it into wine. Buyer beware!

With these legal loopholes and knowing enforcement of a law unpopular in many cities would be challenging, federal agencies were not eager to take on active enforcement of the ban.

Who is going to take care of it?

Existing federal law enforcement entities debated which agency would have the challenge and jurisdiction to enforce this law. The solution was to create a new domestic enforcement unit.

The Bureau of Prohibition was formed to enforce the Volstead Act, and this Bureau bounced between the authority of the Internal Revenue Service to the Department of the Treasury to the Department of Justice, and back to Treasury. The U.S. Coast Guard's waterways enforcement duties held steady throughout the Prohibition years, even as the domestic unit bounced from agency to agency.

∼

SPEAKEASIES GREW

Though home consumption of alcohol was permitted under certain circumstances, citizens still sought out ways to publicly socialize and imbibe.

Illegal taverns, commonly known as speakeasies, and more uncommonly known as blind pigs, could be found in most cities, counties, and towns throughout the United States.

Locations of these establishments were often public secrets, shared through word-of-mouth with whispers of locations and how access could be obtained with a special knock or word given at a guarded door.

The ones called "blind pigs" or "blind tigers" had a unique approach to skirting the law. The name originated from the practice of a business offering customers the opportunity to view a sideshow attraction for a high price while offering a complimentary beverage after the viewing. The attraction could be a blind pig or other oddity.

Attracting customers was an easy challenge compared to maintaining sources of good supply.

The speakeasies needed to tap the unregulated trade in the liquor which meant establishing affiliations with the illegal transport of liquor from the Caribbean and Canada into the United States, as well as with production houses throughout the United States.

When commerce of such a value is unregulated, territories and turfs are carved out by those in the illegal manufacture, importation, and transport businesses. Consequently, an unregulated underground economy fraught with violence and mob influences flourished. Criminal syndicates developed to control the markets in major cities throughout the United States.

Supplies could be uncertain, product quality variable, and the safety of those making the acquisition with large bundles of cash quite perilous.

COCKTAILS BECAME FASHIONABLE

Because of the lack of quality control on liquors, mixed drinks grew in popularity during Prohibition. Much flavoring, sweeteners and fruit garnishes were used to dilute and cover up the taste of lower-quality liquors.

These developed into signature and designer cocktails known throughout the speakeasy culture.

Eventually these cocktails became staples in the well-accepted Americana tradition of the 1950s cocktail hour, and became the foundation for the modern craft cocktail movement.

THE PATHWAY TO REPEAL DAY

The Presidents who served during Prohibition (1920-1933) were, themselves, not strident supporters of the ban.

President Herbert Hoover described Prohibition as "a great social and economic experiment, noble in motive and far-reaching in purpose." And, it's said his wife poured his fine wine collection down the sink the day Prohibition passed.

Though perhaps noble, the experiment ended in failure. Law-abiding companies and establishments capable of making and selling alcohol had been losing money for well over a decade by the time the 18th Amendment was repealed.

Violence, corruption, and the influence of gangsters and underworld syndicates that controlled the liquor trade had grown in major cities throughout the United States.

Impacts on citizens were also widely reported. Physicians saw patients with blindness and neurological damage, such as Jake's Leg palsy and paralysis, from the consumption of tainted bootleg liquor. Patients with these conditions swelled in number to tens of thousands throughout the late 1920s and early 1930s.

Public sentiment had turned.

Repeal Day was heralded December 5, 1933, with final passage of the 21st Amendment to the Constitution. The 21st Amendment stated clearly and succinctly, *"The eighteenth article of amendment to the Constitution of the United States is hereby repealed."*

In 1933, the American trade in liquor emerged from the shadows and out of the hands of criminal elements. Authority was returned to each state to regulate liquor and enact and enforce laws supported by its own citizenry.

Liquor could, theoretically, be sold in all states of the United States, unless a state had its own prohibition and temperance laws on the books, which some did. In fact, Mississippi and Kansas enforced their statewide prohibition laws for decades afterwards.

∼

What follows, in recognition of the 21st Amendment, are the secrets and recipes of 21 cocktails popular in the Roaring Twenties — come travel to when the rules were clear and made to be broken.

BEE'S KNEES

Bee's Knees

The Twenties saw the growth of America's most pronounced and remarkable youthful challenges to culture, marked by young people embracing new fashion, music, dances, language, and freedom.

Young women were rouging their knees and rolling their silk stockings down, shocking behavior for the time. Jazz music and fast dancing became popular, and barriers began to break socially and economically.

The youth culture was reflected in the development of new slang words. The "bee's knees" was 1920s teenage slang for "the best" and, true to it's name, this sweet cocktail may become your best summertime drink.

Because alcohol of any form was scarce, consumers tended to buy whatever they could, from whomever they could, without a strong regard for quality. Acquiring liquor was one challenge; making it palatable was quite another.

Bathtub gin was, however, often less than the best. Prohibition Era cocktails often married honey and lemon juice, as found in the Bee's Knees, to cover the liquor's less than idyllic smell and taste.

With its pretty sugar-rim and simple syrup sweetness, the Bee's Knees remains a favorite cocktail to this day.

.

BEE'S KNEES

2 oz. gin
3/4 oz fresh lemon juice
3/4 oz honey simple syrup (1:1 water to honey)
Lemon twist garnish
Sugar, to rim the glass

Combine gin, lemon juice, syrup, and crushed ice in a cocktail shaker. Shake.
Strain into cocktail glass rimmed with sugar.

Garnish with a lemon twist.

CLOVER CLUB

Clover Club

The Clover Club cocktail dates to 1896 and was rediscovered and reclaimed in the 1920s.

This delightfully elegant drink garnished with fresh raspberries was created by members of the Clover Club, a Philadelphia men's club which met in the Bellevue-Stratford hotel.

Membership in the Clover Club drew from Philadelphia's powerful attorneys, doctors, journalists, and writers who embraced the pink frothy drink along with the club's motto:

> *"Who enters here leaves care behind, leaves sorrow behind, leaves petty envies and jealousies behind."*

This cocktail had a resurgence in the Prohibition Era as the sweet raspberry syrup and pretty, frothy egg white well-covered up a less than perfect bathtub gin.

This cocktail fell from favor after the 1920s, likely due to its complexity of preparation with the double shake the drink requires. Also, the original recipe calls for raw egg whites, which some eschew for fear of contamination with salmonella.

Today, pasteurized egg whites are often substituted for the fresh egg white. This substitution is adequate and does not alter the taste or frothy effect the Clover Club demands.

CLOVER CLUB

1 1/2 oz. gin
1/2 oz. dry vermouth
1/2 oz. lemon juice
1/2 ounce raspberry syrup
1/4 oz. ounce egg white
raspberries, for garnish

Combine gin, vermouth, lemon juice, raspberry syrup and egg white into all cocktail shaker one-fourth full of ice.
Shake until chilled and strain.
Add the liquid back into the cocktail shaker.
Shake again without ice.
Pour the drink into a cocktail glass.

Garnish with a skewer of raspberries.

CORPSE REVIVER - ORIGINAL & NO. 2

Corpse Reviver No. 2

The Corpse Reviver cocktail is a "hare of the dog" drink aimed at returning those who have been over-served to the land of the living.

Some mark this cocktail's origin back to a brief mention of the name in a December 1861 edition of London's *Punch* weekly but Harry Craddock, author of *The Savory Cocktail Book* published in 1930, is credited with the recipe for the Corpse Reviver.

Craddock said of the Corpse Reviver No. 1, *"To be taken before 11 a.m., or whenever steam and energy are needed."* His caution about the Corpse Reviver No. 2. was *"Four of these taken in swift succession will un-revive the corpse again."*

The Corpse Reviver has many variations and the Corpse Reviver No. 2 relied upon a key ingredient that went out of production in the 1960s, Kina Lillet. This wine-based liqueur was created in France in the late 1800s and was flavored with a quinine extract made from Peruvian cinchona bark making it exceedingly bitter.

In the 1960s, a similar but sweeter French liqueur, Lillet Blanc, came to market and the Corpse Reviver No. 2 was again revived.

THE CORPSE REVIVER (ORIGINAL)

1 1/2 oz. brandy
3/4 oz. apple brandy
3/4 oz. sweet vermouth

Combine all ingredients in cocktail shaker.
Fill shaker with ice.
Shake well.
Strain and serve.

∽

CORPSE REVIVER No. 2

1 oz. gin
1 oz. Lillet Blanc
1 oz. orange liqueur
1 oz. lemon juice
1 dash absinthe

Combine all of the ingredients into a cocktail shaker.
Add ice and shake well.
Strain into a chilled glass.

Garnish with a lemon peel twist.

DAIQUIRIS: CLASSIC & FRUITY

Daiquiri, Classic

Few know that the popular Prohibition drink, the Daiquiri, originated in a small Cuban town by the very name.

As documented by the Army-Navy Club, the still-popular daiquiri drink originated in Daiquiri, Cuba.

Daiquiri is in Southeast Cuba, near Guantanamo where American forces first landed in Cuba in 1898 during the Spanish-American War. It is said the drink itself was invented by American mining engineer Jennings Cox.

Daiquiris were a popular drink in Cuba where, until the 1958 Revolution, the world-class rum Bacardi, a daiquiri staple, was manufactured. They were favorite drinks of Ernest Hemingway and President John F. Kennedy.

Included are two daiquiri recipes, the Classic and the Fruity Mango daiquiri.

The Classic daiquiri is a growing rarity; it's popularity having been overtaken by the frozen, fruity concoctions, first made in Havana at the La Floridita Bar by "The King of Cocktails" Constante Ribalaigua Vert.

Fruity, sweet frozen daiquiris have grown in popularity since the 1950s when most post-war American kitchens would be equipped with a blender, and American taste for sweetness grew.

CLASSIC DAIQUIRI

2 1/2 oz. light rum
3/4 oz. fresh squeezed lime juice
1/2 oz. simple syrup (1:1 sugar to water)
Crushed Ice

Add all ingredients to cocktail shaker.
Shake well.
Strain and serve.

∼

FRUITY MANGO DAIQUIRI

1 cup peeled mango, very finely diced
2 Tablespoons fresh lime juice
1 1/2 oz. light rum
1/2 oz. Triple Sec
1 cup crushed ice

Place all ingredients in blender.
Blend until smooth.
Serve.

DUBONNET COCKTAIL

Dubonnet Cocktail

Dubonnet, a fortified French red wine with 15% alcohol by volume, was popular in the 1920s mixed with gin.

Dubonnet itself was created out of a contest by the French government in 1846 to entice members of the French Foreign Legion on North Africa campaigns to take their daily dose of quinine. Quinine was extremely bitter but was a necessary medicine to ward off the malaria prevalent in Africa. When added to wine, troops were more accepting.

This cocktail, first found in Jacques Straub's 1914 book "Drinks," has stood the test of time and is a powerful cocktail-hour favorite, even favored by royalty.

This cocktail is reputed to be a favorite of Queen Elizabeth, who is said to enjoy this as a lunchtime drink, served with two ice cubes.

DUBONNET COCKTAIL

2 oz. gin
2 oz. Dubonnet
1/2 ounce lemon juice
lemon peel twist

Fill a cocktail shaker with ice.
Add gin, Dubonnet, and lemon juice.
Shake well. Strain into a martini glass.
Garnish with lemon twist.

FRENCH 75

French 75

The French 75 is a bubbly, festive drink dubiously named for a piece of World War I battlefield artillery, the French 75mm gun.

The French 75 gun was known for its game-changing power on the battlefield.

Don't underestimate this drink by the same name.

This cocktail dates back to 1922 with its first appearance in Harry MacElhone's *"ABCs of Mixing Cocktails."*

MacElhone, the next year, in 1923, bought Harry's New York Bar in Paris, France, located in the 2nd arrondissement. The bar had been established in 1911 and was a welcome tavern for American soldiers and expats. It has become a legendary Parisian landmark.

In 1924, McElhone began running a "straw poll" of American Presidential elections, allowing any American with proof of citizenship to cast a vote.

For the past 93 years, the votes cast have mirrored the U.S. Presidential election results in all but three of the election years: 1976, 2004 and 2016.

The bar operates to this day, still runs the straw poll, is still in the MacElhone family, and the French 75 is still served.

FRENCH 75

1/2 oz. gin
1/2 oz. lemon juice
3/4 oz. simple syrup
2 oz. chilled champagne

Combine gin, lemon juice and syrup into cocktail shaker.
Fill shaker with crushed ice.
Shake well.
Strain into champagne glass.

Top off with champagne.

GIMLET

Gimlet

The gimlet is a sweet-yet-tart gin drink that has seen a resurgence in popularity over the last decade. Yet, the gimlet's origins, however, are subject to dispute.

The gimlet's creation has been credited to a British naval surgeon, Rear Admiral Sir Thomas Gimlette.

Sir Gimlettete was a physician with a mission - to minimize the risk of scurvy among the Royal Navy on long ocean voyages.

It is said that Sir Gimlette mandated scurvy-preventing lime juice be added to Royal Navy sailors' rations, which included a regular dose of gin.

Others assert the drink's name has an entirely different origin, and credit the cocktail's moniker to a tool by the same name.

In woodworking, a gimlet is a hand tool for drilling small pilot holes in wood without splitting the wood.

The gimlet cocktail, it is said, may have been named for the tool as both have a strong, piercing effect.

Whichever namesake is accurate, the recipe itself is simple, and not disputed.

GIMLET

2 oz. gin
1 oz. Rose's Lime Juice

Combine ingredients in a cocktail shaker filled with ice.
Shake well.
Strain into a chilled cocktail glass.

The gimlet is served without garnish.

GIN RICKEY

Gin Rickey

The Gin Rickey is a quintessential summertime cocktail of gin, lime juice, and club soda created in the 1880s by Colonel Joseph K. Rickey, a Democratic lobbyist, at Shoomaker's Saloon in Washington, D.C.

The Colonel's original recipe called for either whiskey or gin. It is said Colonel Rickey's preference was bourbon.

The gin version of this cocktail became the more popular trend.

Featured in *The Great Gatsby*, the 1925 literary classic by F. Scott Fitzgerald, the Gin Rickey is said to have been Fitzgerald's favorite cocktail.

*I*n *The Great Gatsby*, this cocktail is requested by Daisy when she instructs Tom, her husband, to "make us a cold drink."

Tom leaves the room to make the drink and Daisy takes the opportunity of his absence to kiss Gatsby and profess her love. And the drama begins.

Tom returns carrying *"four gin rickeys that clicked full of ice. Gatsby took up his drink. 'They certainly look cool,' he said with visible tension. We drank in long, greedy swallows"*.

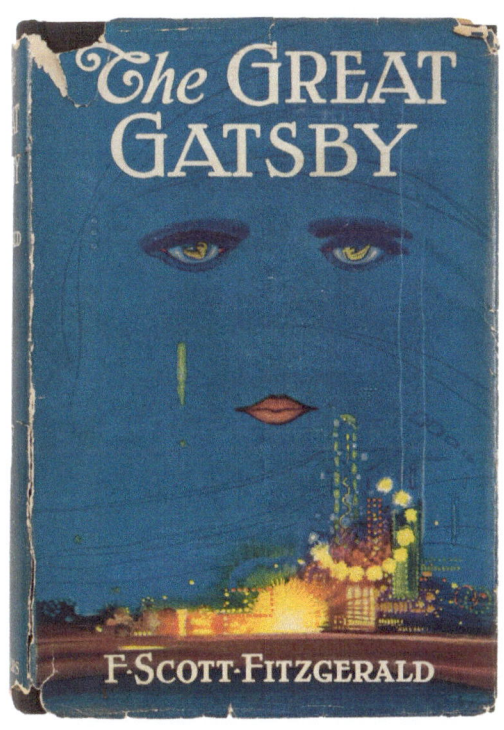

GIN RICKEY

1 1/2 oz. gin
1/2 oz. fresh lime juice
club soda
lime wedge, for garnish

Pour gin and lime juice into a highball glass.
Top with club soda.

Garnish with lime wedge.

HANKY-PANKY

Hanky-Panky

Ada "Coley" Colman, one of the very few female bartenders in the Roaring Twenties not lost to history, crafted the Hanky-Panky, a Prohibition Era favorite.

As a bartender at London's Savoy Hotel, where she served from 1903 to 1925, Coley had a reputation for mixing a good drink and hosting memorable parties.

Only known photograph of Ada Colman tending bar at The Savoy in London

The drink's name has seen a flux in its meaning over the decades.

Today "Hanky-Panky" now hints at dubious intimate activities but in England during the 1920s, the term merely meant "trickery" or "magic."

This cocktail involves a bit of showmanship known as "throwing the drink." Fitting, as Coley first designed this drink for an actor known for his showmanship, Charles Hawtry, who requested Coley make something "with a bit of a punch in it."

At first sip, Hawtry observed, "By Jove! This is the real hanky-panky."

Charles Hawtry, 1911, the first person known to imbibe in the Hanky-Panky

HANKY-PANKY

2 oz gin
1 oz. sweet vermouth
3/4 oz. amaro bitters

Combine ingredients into cocktail shaker.
Add cubed ice.
Throw the Drink.

The Art of Throwing a Drink

"Throwing" the drink chills it without shaking and requires two cocktail shakers.

How to Throw a Drink

- *Pour the drink into a cocktail shaker*
- *Strain liquid into a second ice filled cocktail shaker*
- *First cocktail shaker will have ice remaining in it*
- *Strain the liquid back into the first cocktail shaker*
- *Repeat 4 times moving the liquid back and forth between the two cocktail shakers*

HIGHBALL

Highball

The highball was first created in the late 1800s, and gained popularity during Prohibition due to its complete simplicity.

To make a highball, all one needed was whiskey and a club soda, sarsaparilla, or ginger ale.

By 1950, a "highball" came to mean most any mixed drink, served in a tall glass, comprised of liquor cut with a mixer over ice.

The term "highball" is also the name for the tall straight-sided glass, like a Tom Collins glass, in which a cocktail drink is served.

HIGHBALL

2 oz. whiskey
4 oz. club soda

Fill a highball glass with ice.
Add the whiskey.
Top with club soda.
Serve in a tall (highball) glass.

A Highball is not served with garnish.

MARY PICKFORD

Mary Pickford

With a pretty appearance, this drink is more powerful than it first appears, much like its namesake, Mary Pickford.

Mary Pickford, born Gladys Marie Smith, was a popular silent movie actress who began performing in theaters at age 7 as "Baby Gladys Smith."

Her work ethic and tenaciousness were masked by her gentle smile and engaging demeanor.

Mary Pickford

After "talkies" emerged and her own popularity faded, Mary Pickford did not fade away. Instead, she embraced the business of the film industry and built a legacy which lives on today.

With her husband, actor Douglas Fairbanks, she founded United Artists film studio, and was one of the founders of the Academy of Motion Pictures Arts and Sciences, which created and -to this day- supports the Oscars.

This cocktail was created for Mary during a 1920s trip to Havana, Cuba, which was outside of Prohibition's reach.

MARY PICKFORD

1½ oz. light rum
1½ oz. pineapple juice
¼ oz. grenadine
1 teaspoon maraschino liqueur

Combine ingredients in a cocktail shaker.
Fill shaker with crushed ice.
Strain into a chilled cocktail glass.

Garnish with a brandied cherry.

MINT JULEP

Mint Julep

This bourbon-based cocktail is the official drink of the Kentucky Derby and is most traditionally served in a pewter "julep cup" with a straw. Best enjoyed while wearing a fetching hat watching the race.

Bourbon alone can be a stiff liquor with a bracing after-effect. The muddled mint and sugar in this drink cut the bourbon and make for a refreshing cocktail.

Mint juleps were popular in the 1920s and are featured in the 1925 novel by F. Scott Fitzgerald, *The Great Gatsby*.

The book itself is known as one of the best American novels of the 20th century, though in Fitzgerald's lifetime it had sold poorly and he died believing it a failure.

The Mint Julep made the pages of *The Great Gatsby* in the high-tension chapter where Daisy, Tom and Gatsby are at the Plaza Hotel.

Gatsby claims Daisy doesn't love Tom and Tom exposes Gatsby as a bootlegger. Upset, Daisy just can't hold her tongue.

"Open the whiskey, Tom. I'll make you a mint julep," Daisy tells her husband. *"Then you won't seem so stupid to yourself."*

MINT JULEP

3 oz. bourbon
2 teaspoons simple syrup
8 fresh mint leaves
crushed ice
mint, for garnish

Pour simple syrup into the glass.
Add mint leaves.
Gently bruise with a wooden spoon.
Swipe the sides of the glass with the mint.

Fill glass halfway with crushed ice.
Add bourbon and stir.
Fill glass completely with crushed ice.
Stir until the outside of the glass frosts.

Garnish with sprigs of fresh mint.

MONKEY GLAND

Monkey Gland

The Monkey Gland has a name that begs for the telling of its origin.

The drink first appeared in Harry McElhone's 1922 cocktail guide, *Harry's ABC of Mixing Cocktails*. McElhone was the owner of Harry's New York Bar in Paris.

McElhone is said to have learned of the medical experiments of Dr. Serge Voronoff involving monkey glands and was duly inspired to make a beverage to honor and memorialize the doctor's work.

Dr. Vornoff stunned the 1920s medical community with an unprecedented "rejuvenation" procedure purported to enhance male longevity and performance.

The procedure called for grafting monkey glands to male human testicles.

The medical validity of the rejuvenation claims were found to be dubious and, it is reported, Dr. Vornoff died in obscurity. His drink lives on.

The drink calls for absinthe which in 1912 was banned in the United States, even before Prohibition, and was banned in much of Europe though never in Britain. The bans have since been lifted.

Due to its once scarcity as well as its strong taste, absinthe is often featured in cocktails as a minor additive, or "dash."

MONKEY GLAND

2 oz. gin
1 oz. orange juice
1/4 oz. grenadine
Dash of absinthe
Orange slice for garnish

Swirl the absinthe in a chilled cocktail glass to coat the sides.
Pour out any excess absinthe.
Pour gin, orange juice and grenadine into cocktail shaker.
Add crushed ice and shake well.
Strain into the prepared glass.

Garnish with an orange slice.

PLANTER'S PUNCH

Planter's Punch

A popular Prohibition cocktail, Planter's Punch is an easy summertime indulgence that combines sweet orange juice and a dark rum into a refreshing beverage.

Demand for rum did not fall during Prohibition. As a result, the sugar-growing regions of Cuba, Mexico, and Puerto Rico grew prosperous in the 1920s. These regions found eager markets for their sugar crops, as sugar is a key ingredient in rum.

Rum was an imported liquor much in demand in the Roaring Twenties so much so that "rum-running" came to be shorthand for importation of any liquor by sea into the boundaries of the United States.

The Bahamas became a central shipping point for the rum-runners and the waterways between Florida and the Bahamas became the first "Rum Row." The rum boats would drop anchor outside of U.S. waters and run veritable liquor stores at sea.

To surreptitiously ship rum, it was not uncommon for false bottoms to be built into ships which allowed the product to evade Coast Guard searches.

The Coast Guard responded to the rum-running by expanding its fleet and forces, and soon the Coast Guard had more than 200 enforcement boats to counter the illegal trade.

Rum running ship, Kirk & Sweeney, confiscated by the U.S. Coast Guard in 1924

PLANTER'S PUNCH

2 oz dark rum
1/4 oz grenadine
2 oz. sour mix
2 oz. orange juice
Club soda
Orange slice for garnish

Combine rum, grenadine, sour and orange juice in a glass.
Fill glass with club soda.

Garnish with an orange slice.

SCOFFLAW

Scofflaw

Harry's New York Bar in Paris, the legendary haunt of F. Scott Fitzgerald and Ernest Hemingway, saw the creation of many Prohibition-era cocktails, including the Scofflaw in 1924.

The cocktail is said to have been created in France as a tribute to those who wanted to show their defiance and criticism of U.S. liquor laws. The name itself, however, is a strictly American creation.

This drink quickly made its way across the pond to the States where "scofflaw" itself had been coined as a word only one year before.

The word "scofflaw" resulted from a 1923 contest run by a strict Boston Prohibitionist, Delcevare King.

Delcevare King was a Boston minister and superintendent of the Anti-Saloon League of America. He offered $200 in gold to whoever came up with the best name for a "lawless drinker." Dozens of entries arrived. Two submissions, one by a Miss Kate Butler and one by a Mr. Henry Dale, suggested the word "scofflaw." It is reported they split the winnings and each took home $100 in gold.

The term "Scofflaw" won out over "Boozocrat" and "Boozehevik."

Subsequently, without King's endorsement, the Scofflaw became the moniker of both this forbidden cocktail and those who drank one.

SCOFFLAW

2 oz. bourbon
1 oz. dry vermouth
1/4 oz lemon juice
1/2 oz. grenadine
2 dashes orange bitters

Lemon peel twist for garnish

Add all ingredients but lemon peel to a cocktail shaker.
Fill shaker with ice.
Shake well.
Strain into a chilled cocktail glass.

Garnish with lemon peel twist.

SIDECAR

Sidecar

The sidecar was an emerging mode of transportation in the 1920s and was embraced by the daring youth of the day who wanted the freedom of wheeled transportation but did not have the funds for an automobile.

A London Bucks Club bartender, Pat MacGarry, is credited with creating this drink, as documented in Harry MacElhone's 1922 cocktail guide *Harry's ABC of Mixing Cocktails*.

Popular lore, however, says the Sidecar cocktail was created by a thirsty American Army officer who piloted a motorcycle with a sidecar throughout the streets of London, but whose own name is lost to history.

The Sidecar was a fitting name for a cocktail that was breaking new ground, as were those who dared ride in a sidecar.

The motorcycle version of a sidecar was first patented in 1903 by Mr. W. J. Graham of the Graham Brothers out of Middlesex, England. The sidecar's popularity grew throughout the 1920s and then dropped during the Depression years.

Today the cocktail is seen more often than is a motorcycle sidecar, which took special skill to safely navigate.

SIDECAR

1 1/2 oz. bourbon
3/4 oz. cointreau
3/4 oz. lemon juice
lemon peel twist for garnishing
Sugar, for rimming glass

Pour bourbon, cointreau and lemon juice
into cocktail shaker.
Add ice.
Shake well.
Strain into cocktail glass rimmed with sugar.

Garnish with lemon peel twist.

SOUTH SIDE

South Side

The South Side is reputed to have been the favorite cocktail of Al Capone who ruled the South side of Chicago during the 1920s, and is said to have been first created at the 21 Club in New York.

Al Capone, May 16, 1929 Philadelphia Department of Corrections photograph

The South side's Al Capone earned a reputation as one of the United States' youngest, most notorious gangsters, and a kingpin of illegal liquor trafficking during the Prohibition Era.

Notably, he served no time for his reputed role in Chicago's 1929 Saint Valentine's Day Massacre which left seven men gunned down in broad daylight. Never arrested for any role in the Massacre, Capone was jailed in Philadelphia several months later for carrying a concealed, unlicensed gun.

Capone's influence waned when, at age 33, he was jailed for tax evasion. He died at age 48 in Palm Island, Florida.

SOUTH SIDE

Fresh mint leaves, torn and bruised
1 1/2 oz. gin
3/4 oz. lemon juice
1/2 oz. simple syrup
club soda
lemon peel twist and mint for garnish

Combine mint, gin, juice and syrup in cocktail shaker.
Add cracked ice.
Shake.
Strain into a highball glass filled with ice.
Top off with club soda.

Garnish lemon twist and mint sprig.

THE LAST WORD

The Last Word

𝒯he Last Word is a pretty cocktail with its pour of green chartreuse, and has a disputed origin.

This cocktail is said to have been created in Detroit at the Detroit Athletic Club where it first appeared on a menu in 1916.

Others attribute its origins to American vaudevillian performer the "Dublin Minstrel," Frank Fogarty, who performed in New York but occasionally visited Detroit, and is reputed to have enjoyed "the last word" in conversations.

𝒯his cocktail makes for a colorful drink with a strong bouquet due to its unique mix of Green Chartreuse, lime juice and maraschino liqueur.

Green Chartreuse is a rare liqueur with a big secret. This colorful liquid has been made by Carthusian Monks since 1737. It's recipe is held closely and is known to only the two monks charged with its manufacture at any one time.

Procuring this liqueur may require a hunt and it can be found at finer liquor stores.

THE LAST WORD

3/4 oz. gin
3/4 oz. Green Chartreuse
3/4 oz. maraschino liqueur
3/4 oz. lime juice

Combine all ingredients into a cocktail shaker.
Fill with ice and shake well.
Strain into a cocktail glass and serve.

Garnish with a twist of lime peel.

TUXEDO NO. 2

Tuxedo No. 2

*F*itting there would be a Prohibition cocktail dedicated to the opulent class of men who could afford to own and don a fine tuxedo.

The Roaring Twenties were a time of abundance and decadence, with money abounding. Formal parties and attire set the social scene, especially in New York.

The tuxedo itself, as formalwear, was named for the moneyed set of New York's Tuxedo Park, and is said to have been introduced from England to the United States at the neighborhood's exclusive Tuxedo Club.

The tuxedo has since became attire of formal occasions throughout the Western world.

When one should wear a tuxedo, and what kind - whether black or white, whether boxcar or swallow-tailed - became the subject of often unspoken rules.

Emily's Post seminal 1922 work *Etiquette*, which came to be known as the "Blue Book of Social Usage," established these and other social conventions. Her book was based on what she observed inside the Tuxedo Park neighborhood's storied stone gates and within its Tuxedo Club.

The original drink, the Tuxedo, was created first in 1903 and called for maple gin, not commonly available across the United States. An adaptation was made and the Tuxedo No. 2 recipe was developed using dry gin.

TUXEDO NO. 2

2 oz. dry gin
3/4 oz. dry vermouth
1/4 oz. maraschino liqueur
2 dashes orange bitters
Absinthe, for coating the glass
Lemon peel twist, for garnish

Rinse the inside of a chilled cocktail glass with absinthe.
Pour off excess absinthe.
Combine gin, vermouth, maraschino and orange bitters in cocktail shaker filled with crushed ice.
Strain into chilled glass.

Garnish with a lemon twist.

TWELVE-MILE LIMIT

Twelve-Mile Limit

The Twelve-Mile Limit Prohibition Era cocktail took its name from the extended reach of U.S. Prohibition laws into territorial waters as of 1924.

Lawmakers knew the reach of the law needed to extend beyond the land of the United States and into waterways lest Prohibition be easily circumvented by creative boaters.

Initially, the law mandated a three-mile buffer around the United States within which one could neither serve nor transport liquor.

The three-mile buffer was rooted in history, as it was the range a cannon fire could reach.

When Prohibition began, all ships bearing liquor within the three-mile zone ran the risk of being boarded and confiscated by the U.S. Coast Guard.

Lawmakers' intent was thwarted when illegal liquor traders realized it was possible to row a boat a bit more than three miles out to sea, purchase liquor from an awaiting ship, and return to U.S. shores with a rowboat full of liquor.

Though an intriguing and daring undertaking, such dramatic action was actually not a strong contributor to the illegal sale of alcohol during Prohibition. In truth, no more than 2% of liquor sold during

Prohibition was actually smuggled into the country. The majority was produced within the States illegally.

Nonetheless, the law was changed in April 1924 to extend the boundary waters of the United States to a twelve-mile limit, beyond what a person could row — and, thereafter, a fine cocktail name came to be.

TWELVE-MILE LIMIT

1 oz. rum
1/2 oz. rye whiskey
1/2 oz brandy
1/2 oz. grenadine
1/2 oz. lemon juice
Lemon peel twist for garnish

Combine all ingredient but lemon peel
into a cocktail shaker filled with ice.
Shake until well chilled.
Strain into a cocktail glass.

Garnish with a lemon peel twist.

WARD 8

Ward 8

The Ward 8 cocktail was created in 1898 to recognize the election of Martin Lomasney to the General Court of Massachusetts, the state's governing body.

Lomasney had held governance over Boston's West End for fifty years, serving as an alderman, state representative, and then state Senator. He was known for a commitment to create housing, employment, and social and cultural opportunities for new immigrants, thereby establishing their trust and loyalty.

In that process, Lomasney earned the nickname "The Mahatma of Ward 8" for his ability to reliably deliver the Ward 8's vote for Democratic party candidates.

Lomasney is remembered as a consummate politician and his guidance to politicians lives on today. He instructed fellow politicians —

"Never write if you can speak; never speak if you can nod; never nod if you can wink."

The Ward 8 cocktail, though first created before the turn of the century, had a strong resurgence during Prohibition and is popular still.

The cocktail's sweet grenadine and fragrant orange and lemon juices combined to sweeten a rough bootleg whiskey, making for a smooth drink.

WARD 8

2 oz. rye whiskey
3/4 oz. lemon juice
3/4 oz. orange juice
3/4 teaspoon grenadine
Seltzer water

Combine whiskey, lemon juice, orange juice, and grenadine in a cocktail shaker.

Fill shaker with ice and shake well.
Strain into a chilled highball glass filled halfway with ice.
Top off with seltzer.

Ward 8 is not served with a garnish.

NOTICE TO THE PUBLIC
=AND TO ALL=
DEALERS IN LIQUORS
We have notified (through the Press) all dealers in liquors that we own and control the brand
"WARD 8"
which we have protected by Registration throughout the United States. Any infringement on the above brand will be prosecuted by the   SANTA CLARA COMPANY,
No. 159 Washington St.,
Boston, Mass.
Perfection reached in the Art of Compounding.
The Newest, Latest and Up-to-Date drink.
If your dealer cannot supply you, send directly to us.
The price of "Ward 8" is $1.00 a Bottle, $10.00 a Case.

The Ward 8 liquor name was claimed by the Santa Clara Company of Boston

1920S COCKTAIL PARTY PLANNER

What's a 1920s cocktail without a party?

All you need are a few tempting bites, good music, plenty of crushed ice, delightful drinks + dear friends

Please remember to advise guests to drink only in moderation and not to drink and drive.

A good host should serve only nonalcoholic beverages toward the end of a party and always anticipate the need of, and arrange for, alternative transportation in advance.

Included here are the hors d'oeuvres popular in the 1920s, a shopping list for liquid refreshments, photo booth prop ideas, select popular Roaring Twenties tunes, and a notes section for your own ideas.

ROARING TWENTIES HORS D'OEUVRES

Crab Stuffed Mushrooms
Oysters Rockefeller
Salmon Mousse on Toast Points
Shrimp Cocktail

Crudités and Radish Roses
Cucumber Canapés
Deviled Eggs
Olives and Nuts Tray

Fresh Fruit Tray
Mini Lemon Cakes

COCKTAILS SHOPPING LIST

Liquors

Absinthe
Aromatic Bitters
Bourbon
Brandy
Champagne
Cointreau
Dubonnet
Gin

Green Chartreuse
Grenadine
Lillet Blanc
Maraschino Liqueur
Orange Bitters
Rum, light and dark
Rye
Vermouth, dry and sweet
Triple Sec
Whiskey

∽

Nonalcoholic Beverages

Club Soda
Colas & Diet Colas
Iced Tea
Lemonade
Limeade
Orange Juice
Pineapple Juice
Raspberry Syrup
Seltzers
Sour Mix
Sparkling Water
Still Water
Tonic

∽

Garnishments and Additives

Egg Whites (pasteurized)
Lemons
Limes
Mangoes
Mint
Orange
Raspberries

PHOTO BOOTH PROP IDEAS

Bow Ties
Cigarette Holders
Chalkboard and Chalk
Champagne Bottle & Glasses
Cloche Hats
Cigars
Feather Boas
Fedoras
Gloves, Opera-length
Headbands with Feathers or Sequins
Raccoon Coat
Strands of Pearls
Tuxedo Jackets
Tweed Newsboy Caps

POPULAR ROARING TWENTIES SONGS

Ain't Misbehavin' - Fats Waller (1929)
Ain't She Sweet - Piccadilly Revels Band (1927)
Black Bottom - Howard Lanin (1926)
Charleston - Tennessee Tooters (1925)
Down' the Raccoon - George Olsen & His Music (1928)
Down My Way - Jelly Roll Norton (1929)
I've Found a New Baby - Ted Lewis & His Band (1926)
Montain Dew - Bascom Lamar Lunsford (1928)
Swanee - Al Jolson (1920)
Sweet Georgia Brown - Ben Bernie & His Orchestra (1921)
Yes Sir! That's My Baby - Gene Austin (1925)
West End Blues - Louis Armstrong & His Hot Five (1928)

∼

PARTY PLANNING NOTES

_____
_____
_____
_____
_____
_____
_____
_____

Dear Reader,

Thank you for reading *Prohibition Cocktails* and letting me share some of the history of the Roaring Twenties.

If you enjoyed *Prohibition Cocktails*, please consider leaving a review on *Amazon*. Reviews are very, very important to authors and I'd be delighted to hear from you. Just clicking the Stars helps greatly.

This book is a companion to the *Somewhere Still*, a novel set in the Roaring '20s in a town alive with speakeasies, jazz and scandal. Come travel to a time when the rules were clear and made to be broken.

Thanks so much!

Denitta

If you're interested in advance news of new releases, please sign up for my newsletter at www.denitta.com.

ALSO BY DENITTA WARD

Somewhere Still

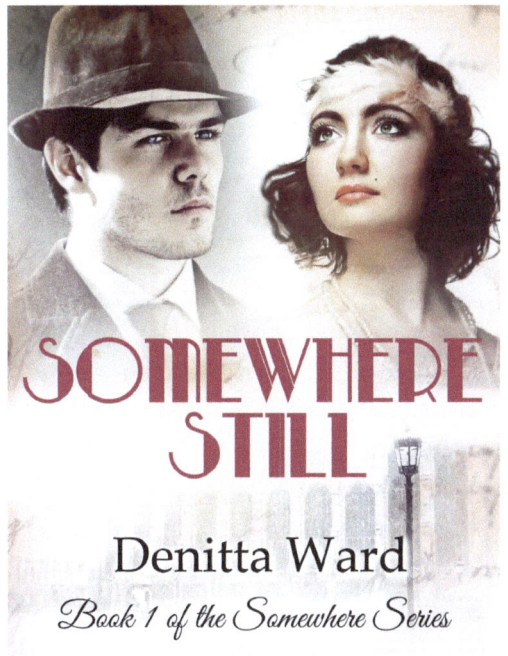

Come on a journey to the scandalous Roaring Twenties when the rules were clear and made to be broken.

Buy it now on Amazon and Barnes & Noble.

Somewhere Still, coming-of-age Roaring Twenties historical fiction, is the story of one young woman's transformative journey of love, betrayal, and redemption, and the power of women when they band together.

From the day Jean Ball lands a job at the elegant Empire hotel, she quickly learns the secrets of the entitled class. Dazzled by a Roaring Twenties society on the cusp of radical change, this naive and innocent young woman finds herself dancing, bobbing her hair, and falling for Elden Whitcomb, the handsome son of the wealthy hotel owner. The stakes rise when the Whitcombs' powerful secrets are revealed and loving Elden comes at a price – one that may be too high for Jean to pay.

Shattered and alone, Jean's in the battle of her life in a city alive with romance, smoky speakeasies, jazz music and scandal, but divided by race and class. With the help and encouragement of influential women, Jean may find what she has always needed, though her choices could echo through generations. But will the man she trusted and so fiercely loves redeem himself?

Ward uses historical sites and real events to explore Jean's transformation from an innocent young girl to a self-assured woman, making her way in a society in transition.

Somewhere Still gives insight into 1920s Kansas City, a city on the cusp of significant change. During this time, the city's society women united to urge social advances, the jazz culture was born, baseball's famous Negro League was formed, and the city was awash with scandal from the burgeoning Prohibition bootleg trade.

Kirkus Reviews calls this debut novel "well done" and a "vivid portrait of Kansas City in the 1920s."

Buy *Somewhere Still* now on Amazon and Barnes & Noble.

ABOUT THE AUTHOR

Denitta Ward, author of the Somewhere Series, writes historical fiction and captures history from the foothills of the Rocky Mountains. She is a member of the Women's Fiction Writers Association, the Historical Novel Society, and Rocky Mountain Fiction Writers.

For the latest news and book releases, sign up for Denitta's Newsletter at www.denitta.com.

- facebook.com/Denittawrites
- twitter.com/denittaward
- instagram.com/denittaward
- goodreads.com/denittaward
- amazon.com/author/denittaward
- bookbub.com/authors/denittaward
- pinterest.com/ddward0596

PHOTO CREDITS

Prohibition Cocktails: 21 Secrets & Recipes

All Cocktail Photography by Kent Ward (2018)

Author Photo by Nicole Jenkins (2017)

Other photographs are in the Public Domain.

www.ingramcontent.com/pod-product-compliance
Lightning Source LLC
Chambersburg PA
CBHW041508010526
44118CB00006B/186